I WILL NOT FALL

I WILL NOT FALL

SARAH GALE

&

TEGAN GIGANTE

Published in 2013
as a Tinder Press / Philovox collaboration.

Sarah Gale: sistermud@gmail.com

Tegan Gigante: birdfish@live.com.au

COVER IMAGE
Landscape with the Fall of Icarus
by Pieter Brueghel the Elder

ISBN-13: 978-1484958537

ISBN-10: 1484958535

CONTENTS

SARAH GALE

Sing to Me 9
Excuse Me 10
God Loves a Campfire 12
Odin 13
Let the Machinery Take Over 15
A Beautiful Lie 17
The Invisible Ones 18
On Your Lonely Road 20
A Fire can be a Foul Thing 22
The Garden 26

TEGAN GIGANTE

First Light in Blank Verse 29
Sutra 30
Desire 31
Hymn to Nye 32
Like Fire 34
Little Things 35
Rain on a Tin Roof 36
(*Neither Wet nor Dry*) 37
The Myriad Things 38
Nasturtiums 39
My Days 42
For Sarah 44
I Will Not Fall 46
Death 47
Forgive Me 49

SARAH GALE

Sing to Me

Sing to me of cobwebs cupped
   to bleeding mouths
and rocks that wail at midnight,
   sing to me

Sing to me of trees that swallow
   children who stray too close
and birds that become women
   when they are wooed

Excuse Me

Yesterday the transitional man
lit his fag at my fingertips.
His face rippled in the flame;
he boasted a phosphorous sheen
like neon reflected in the
Yarra's dirty foil.

He spoke, I suppose,
as human candles do
in a tectonic mumble
—— he sheltered moths
in his mouth
and would not drink
for fear of tiny ghosts

he said *excuse me*,
he said *excuuuse me*,
I seem to have something
lodged inside my head,
a dirty bird —— an aping shadow
that I can't quite get
my fingers round

sure, I said
who am I to deny
a shining man?
Perhaps I can pluck
that strange light free

—— I would be an avatar too
and rob him
of his angelic decline.

So I grasped
that incandescence
and I pulled
that strange light free,
I had it in my fingers,
it was perfect as a tooth

and I saw my aping shadow
flung up high in gelid hunger;
it rained upon his shining brow
—— he opened wide,
the moths flew out,
the dust of many wingtips
sifted gently in my mouth

I said *excuse me*
I said *excuuuse me*

God loves a campfire

Those tiny lights separated
in the dark

—— he created the Lurk and the Loom
for a very good reason

so that we may prevaricate
somewhere in between

—— learn the beauty
of truth's shadow animals

hey presto,
prestidigitation

—— the crowd applauds
indignantly

Odin

The raven god bides with his pets
beneath the ghost train
— old one eye laid out,
ravens curled dumb at his ears,
nestled amongst the rubbish,
amongst the rubble
that seeps between the tracks

flat on his back
he imagines backstroking blood
thick with sacrifice
and smiles with the screams
of the marks above him.
Almost like old times;
enough for him to rest
and trust to reawaken,
godhood intact.

As dog sometimes, he leaves and prowls
and laps at sticky fingers,
noses popcorn loose from rubbish bins;
the carny folk seem to know him,
but have tired of divinity
— he yips and howls at a thrown toffee apple
and skulks within the shadows.

The children know him too,
and those lost lonely fools who prowl
at humanity's outskirts

—— once a girl offered her skinned knee
and Odin blinked his one bright eye at her,
she lifted her skirt and her warm, red blood
tasted like old times.

Wotan, she whispered,
as she flashed him a glimpse of her underpants.

This is something that he chooses to remember,
he has learnt some tricks
some sleight of hand from these
modern nomads and their herds.

Old one eye
chooses his memories carefully now;
this modern world offers no recompense
for vengeance, for glory, for the birth of gods,
for men who rise up from the dead.
Better to dream and scrounge and wait
for the world's end and the wolf Fenrir.

The sun sets on his back, brindle and gold,
and affords him some of his lost glory.
Odin snaps a rat in two and
accepts its feeble offering

whilst Fenrir's chain
pulls taut
and vermin gnaw
at the root of *Ygdrasil,* the world tree.

Let the machinery take over

Let the machinery take over,
let it love her if it may,
her metal paramour
with blood in its gears.
She feels nothing.

Let it frighten the dead
with its mechanical roaring
like a dull bird at day's end calling,
calling, for unspeakable rut.

Let it love her if it may
bracketed by the earliest stars
fractured into lurid hallucinations of colour
spilled red, or the yellow of subcutaneous fat

there is no gentle place
where it may lay her down,
her body cannot comfort
flat planes and corners
nor receive it;
she feels nothing.

Let it love her if it may
in the galaxial black
of a starving child's eye
a night for love or murder, she thinks
as it grinds down those small things
she once cossetted, beneath it,

she is strung somehow between;
and here's the trick,
she feels nothing but the faintest
    dew upon her skin
and the imprints of machinery

teasing her body
till it is a facsimile
of itself, a collection
of strings and pulleys
housed within a tender sleeve.

Desire will eventually seize the circuitry
in a hopeless continuum,
wires and tendons mutate into a rictus
of assumed life

together, they will become an instrument
from which she can pluck free tunefulness,
so that she may be a bard
to her own, soft-fleshed kind

of the love that feels like
nothing much at all

A Beautiful Lie

I want to say that love has redeemed me
I want to say that hope lives like a small polite
animal in the woodwork of the world,

I want to say that rocks are just
that birds are prayers and
the grass sings hymns
when the wind blows across it,

I want to say that beauty lives on my tongue
and that everything I taste
holds something of the wonder
    of the world in it.

I want to say love has redeemed me.
I want to say something so beautiful
that it is a lie

The Invisible Ones

When the invisible ones
have sloughed off their skins for new,
dimmer hides
and we like fools assume them gone
like the light in a dying man's eyes,
less somehow,
obscured by an editor's brush

the unwelcome whisper,
strange and uninvited
attributable only to those guilty
moments we imagine
tugging at our ropes, branding us
here-now, here-now
where the stomach growls
and mouth belches
and minds sicken with each dreary plot

with the periphery of shadow carnivores
panting at our wakes to bite and
sometimes take from us that dearest,
that love, that conquers us.
How jealously we guard our treasures.

For the sake of artifice
we pretend knowledge
for the love of truth
our dreams ridicule us,

how we reveal ourselves for a moment
and then quickly quash the revelatory.
Instead, we slow our pace and tip our heads
as if a momentary madness draws
those invisible ones near with their hounds.

With their whispers.

On Your Lonely Road

I have packed a basket,
watch your fingers
watch your fingers

if you become hungry and grasp
for the thick smell
for the dead smell
enlivened by flame

if you become thirsty
for the bottle that peeps
sly and winkled
from the napkins

—— remember that the wolf
holds claim
on the basket too
and that your hand,
soft and forgetful,
does not necessarily love you

it has made its allegiance
with the wicker god
with the brand
with the sickle,
with the red cloth
darned and decorated
by lost children

and with the wildflowers,
doomed for their
transient beauty

A Fire Can Be a Foul Thing

A fire can be a foul thing
when it has burst free of story time
— burst free of night time
when the hounding of hours
rages on the periphery
till they lay their dusty heads in sleep

when fire, in dire imitation of its father
thrusts itself outward, seeking mates
seeking names, places
within which to gestate
a greater constellation…

You could almost pity its rude desire,
licking the absence in between
for a shred of shared breath,
a tinder of affection
if it weren't for its despotic claim
upon everything that has
a face or space to lay roots in,

the sky assumes a mask in wry concession
winking one dry eye — the sun, the father
diminished from here
by its son's hubris: a bloodshot orb
displacing shadows, obscured
by an ashen haze

jealousy informs its colour

I am the sky god
I am the original flame

seized by Loki and brought down
to this unhallowed place
where men and women burn for pleasure
where men and women burn for light –
the golden mean upon which their souls travel,
the sons of suns

Loki a mother to this wayward son,
— sly in his rustling skirts
of dry grass and rotten tree limbs
is also father to the iron workers,
the conjurors of steel and atom bombs
— his fox face flash-burnt and intent
upon mischief.

No, the sky will not be shed of its little sons,
its tyrannous offspring,
they must always return glutted and angry —
as my skin shall not be shed
of these tiny brown constellations,
these stars in negative

my skin may be an astrologer's chart
of stellars and melanomas, phenomena
that will die with me, untouched by a star's
true melancholy insistence to shine,
    prey only to a time

I cannot encompass, without losing
      what humanity
I have gathered about me like rough hides,
the bones of my descendants piled beneath me;

they are bared to no vision of light
they are crowded beneath my living body,
an altar upon which I too must succumb;
      and dumb,
await a new sacrifice to drench my weary sticks,
to hold off the flames, the ash oblivion
for another generation.

Fire can be a foul thing, exiled from
      the father body;
it has learnt appetite
it has a mouth, bright teeth
and a tongue it flaps in desperate succour
for a kindly breast that it can only
      scorch and blacken
with its need

—— so blood and sap will have to do
yes, blood and sap will have to do
and the ghosts of a million nursery rhymes
will sing from the ashes

I was once
I was once
I was once

a flame in the garden of light

Not all of us are sons or suns
or enamoured of the light of day, of flame
or flesh.

May the stars cease their chatter
may those sly interpreters,
that gaudy panoply that wink and flail
take our places on the altar
and leave us free to be consumed
by older appetites

I was once
I was once
I was once

a shadow in the forest of night
and the moon's mild light, though borrowed,
begs a gentler gaze
held in rapport with lakes and mirrors,
a softer breast
upon which to lay our appetites

The Garden

We meet between the pinnacles,
press ourselves into
warm pink meat

bury our faces
in that florid first breath
and dream of a garden
paired, perfected
behind our ribs:

our harlequin dreamings
deny the litter of bones
that hedge us in

TEGAN GIGANTE

First light in blank verse

She wakes and scopes the forming world.
The shadows move, prepare to flee,
as violet sky shakes loose of night.
In her room, dusty windows show
tall trees touch light, the first to reach
this landing day. She waits and hopes
that morning will hand down the sun.

Sutra

The thread binds;
connects the thought
to the word.

The thread stitches
the shape of letters
into the page.

The thread reaches
out from the poem,
warping into your weft.

The thread joins
what is ready to become
with the world of becoming.

The thread heals
the division of flesh,
sealing two parts into one.

The thread intersects;
marks the shift
from point to web.

The thread bridges
the invisible city of poetry
to my own poor house.

Desire

I will knit myself into you:
with my own teeth for needles
and your need as thread
I will make this binding tight.
There may be places where your skin is thick,
times when my will is weak,
but I will push and coax the means
    to hold you here
and will not relent.

…And when I find I am no longer sewing
    but sewn,
I may fight to break free.
I may unstitch your heart to find myself again.

Hymn to Nye

Darkness is more
than merely absence of light:
it is made by the shapes
of enclosing spaces,
the curve of the world
to hide half of herself
from the sun;
the contours of hills and valleys;
the myriad light-seeking beings
that themselves cast a shadow,
shades of the light
they have consumed.

The night is not yet dark,
nor still nor silent enough;
we seek our homes, our beds,
a deeper womb in which
to wrap ourselves in shelter
from the too-bright stars,
the ever-active moon.

We know the chasm of the interior –
the promise of receipt
and the woman who receives –
not only by her doors and rooms
but by her curves,

by the outward roundness
that suggests – implies –
her hidden spaces.

We love the mountain
for her mysteries,
for her hidden caves,
and always
for her undeniable
presence.

Like Fire

Hold it closer:
Your words fall like fire
On my loose-brained tongue

Sing it harder:
Each note plays to my flesh
And I would die to answer

If I had the music

Little things

It's the little things
that keep me here,
that string the days along
between the flashes;
to tide the time
between the joy;
between those flickering moments
of elation and lucidity ——
Oh I could not sustain the breath
that is caught on an epiphany;
I take small mouthfuls each day
of the details, the delicacy
of a snail shell or
the exquisite lines
that form a purple cabbage

Rain on a tin roof

. . .

falling like

rain

      on a

  tin   roof

always falls:

off-beat,
amplified,
hitting hard
and wet
and shapeless,

Rain on a tin roof

falling on

my dry house
and my
hot wet tea inside
my dry skin
and my
hot wet blood inside

(Neither Wet nor Dry)

Some light
has bled
along this shaft
and dripped with
slow
deliberate
ease
upon the skin
that binds me here:

the need
to turn my face,
to bare my eyes
and will the drop
to flow in flood,
has caught the light
in frozen stare

leaving nothing lit
except my need

The Myriad Things

My touch moments upon
a thousand things
which include you
and the vast sky

in each instant
the myriad things
shift and shape-change
in a thousand directions
which include many ways down
and the vast sky

my touch lights upon
the myriad details
of this detail-rich world
and is still hungry

Nasturtiums
for Gwen Harwood

Lines: you revisit me now
like a new wind, or
an old breath breathed again,
and this time I feel the death
that stilled your wild mind.

You no longer move your shapes
across the page — as to each —
such intimate arrangements.
I do not seek to shadow
the dance of grace you left
as etchings on your grave;
and — as to each — must hope
to foster traceries, to
shape my own designs.

The breath that moved
your words was yours alone, and
— as to each — such secret alchemy
occurred within your warm body
as it was then
a spell to change ephemera
of thought and air
to spoken breath, to tempered
forms of woven gold…
The pattern of your moulds
are broken, unrepeatable.

I repeat the experiment
and my alembic spawns
such different forms,
upon pages as white and clean
as your own once were.

Outside my window
wild nasturtiums bloom,
their colour lifting me
from the encroaching gloom,
the autumn sky a grey premonition
of winter and of death.
Between your time and mine,
the pattern of the floating leaves
and timely shape of flowers
has been kept, repeated,
while yours did not survive the winter;
is instead preserved in fragile parchment,
an artefact voiced in the throats of strangers.
In the wake of so many minds dead,
our flowering must be made anew;
poets must populate each spring
and from the same air
breathe new shapes.

Somehow I will be gone,
just as you are now;
and — as to each —

our letters will be equal lost
to new winds, and new deaths.
And on some yet unimagined earth,
the same nasturtiums still may bloom,
their colours cut across the room to find
the eyes of some yet unimagined mind.

My Days

My days are for
watching the sky,
not expecting portents
but to marvel at the moon;
for basking in the single
sun and simply being
the one at the centre
of vast stars
wheeling in their course.

My days are for
feeling the roots of my toes
and the palms of my feet
flow into the earth
so there is no space
between my body
bound in skin
and everything else.

My days are for
knowing the thrum of blood
in all the corners and curves;
the length and contraction
of muscle as I move.

My days are for
pulling air into lungs
and exhaling
my very self
into the mattering
of things

For Sarah

A moment distilled
from so many:
pink baling twine
under a new moon
plucked from my pocket
tangled in keys -
your unimaginably
beautiful daughter
cradled on my hip
distilled, in this moment,
at four years old -
we manage to bind
the twine around a
blue and white
mushroom box,
in the dark of which
crouches a lonely hen,
the only survivor
of a fox raid,
now a refugee
from your house to mine.

All our tragedies, our
private moments of despair,
our soft, child-like fears,
have seen us grow older
in our different ways,

but we are distilled
together in this moment,
three conspirators
come close to whisper
in the night.

I will not fall

I will not fall for love again
I will not fall for love
I will not fall
I will not

Death

I.

Death: it is my turn to say
that in the face of your long lapses
I have read vital marks
upon certain graves:
and so the dead have spoken
despite you.
The signs are fading,
they are bowing before you
in your guise as
God of fragmentation,
as everything must

and despite you words are spoken,
again, and the same again,
and when forgotten
will be remembered again

II.

Death: it is my turn to hope
that when you take me
you take the stuff of my stay,
all the debris and entanglements
that I have been keeping from you.

Dissolve the bridges,
holy and broken and worn;
unmake the ripples
I have sent into the world —

then I will worship you
and no other

Forgive me

Never have I met you
on the right ground;
never have I matched, intact,
intent to movement;
never have my gestures
seemed to give enough;
never have my phrases
pinned exactly what
I hoped to say.

On the birthday of the world
I failed to find the right gift.

Always I have wanted
to look you in the eye;
always I have tried
to play true notes;
always I have meant
to reach out my hands;
always I have sought
to find essential words:

Next year,
on the birthday of the world
I will try again to find the right gift.

Made in the USA
Monee, IL
07 July 2026